Learn Go

A Comprehensive Beginners Guide to Learning Go

Koso Brown

Contents

Introduction

Google's Go programming language, which has been available for more than a decade, has changed from being a curiosity for tech enthusiasts to the robust programming language used in some of the most significant cloud-native software projects worldwide.

Although Go, also known as Golang, was developed by Google staff members, primarily Rob Pike, a notable engineer at Google and a veteran Unix expert, it is not officially a "Google project." Instead, Go is an open-source project that is being developed by the community, with strong leadership guiding the language's future direction and how it should be utilized.

Go is designed to be easy to use, simple to learn, and easy for other developers to read. Go's feature set is somewhat small, especially in comparison to other programming languages like C++. Because of its syntax, which is similar to that of C, Go is relatively simple for experienced C developers to understand. Nevertheless, a lot of Go's features—particularly its functional programming and concurrency features—are reminiscent of Erlang and other older languages.

Go shares many similarities with Java as a C-like language for creating and managing cross-platform enterprise applications of various kinds. You might also compare Go and Python to facilitate the quick construction of code that might execute anywhere, but the distinctions between the two languages are much more than the similarities.

" quick, statically typed, compiled language that feels like a dynamically typed, interpreted language" is how the Go documentation characterizes Go. Even a big Go program can be compiled in a few seconds. Additionally, Go does not have as much overhead as C-style includes files and libraries.

Chapter 1

The history of Go

Go was developed by Google as a C++ substitute to address its software engineering problems. Additionally, as multicore computers gained popularity at the time, a language with improved productivity levels was required.

In 2007, Google started working on the Go design. The goal of the Go programming language's creators was to provide a more user-friendly language with all of the beneficial features of other languages, such as C++, Python, and JavaScript. In 2009, Go was introduced as an open-source project that allowed community members to work together on concepts and code. Later in 2012, version 1.0 was made available.

New features and upgrades have been added throughout time, like generics in 2022. Because Go is utilized by well-known businesses like Google, Cloudflare, Dropbox, MongoDB, Netflix, SoundCloud, Twitch, and Uber, its popularity has only increased.

What is the Go/Golang programming language?

Google created the open-source programming language Go, commonly known as Golang or Go language. Software developers can create online applications, cloud and networking services, and other kinds of software using Go in a variety of operating systems and frameworks.

Go is an explicit, statically typed programming language inspired by C. Go has gained popularity for creating microservices and other applications because of its quick startup time, minimal runtime overhead, and ability to function without the need for a virtual machine (VM). Go is also used for concurrent programming, which is the practice of carrying out several tasks concurrently, either partially or not at all.

Python's simplicity and productivity served as an inspiration for the creation of the Go language. For effective dependency management, goroutines—lightweight processes—and a set of packages are utilized. It was created to address several issues, such as cross-language development, sluggish build times, unmanaged dependencies, effort duplication, and difficulties creating automated tools.

4

What is the function of the Go programming language?

For software development, Go teams utilize the following aspects of the language:

➢ Lightweight goroutines that function similarly to threads and a channel system that enables communication between goroutines form the foundation of a concurrency model. The grammar of the code follows basic patterns found in dynamic languages, giving preference to composition interfaces over inheritance. This makes it possible for programmers to create applications that can handle several tasks at once.

➢ Go's modular design allows for code to be compiled on nearly any platform thanks to its platform independence.

➢ Unit tests, which enable debugging and quality assurance while running concurrently with written code, are one type of testing support.

➢ A type system that guarantees conversions and compatibility while avoiding problems associated with dynamically typed languages is provided by static typing.

➢ Code package management makes it possible to

publish packages with a limited number of commands and to manage both external and user-created code packages.

➤ A standard library facilitates the addition and use of new functionality in code by utilizing distributed packages as its foundation.

Some of Go's tools are as follows:

➤ Go build assembles Put dependencies and packages for Go into an executable library.

➤ Go, vet, look at Examine the source code for errors and questionable structures.

➤ Godoc creates documentation using Hypertext Markup Language based on the code structure and developer comments.

➤ Go test allows code testing and performance data collection by running benchmarks and unit tests.

➤ Gofmt automatically reads code by formatting and indenting it.

➤ Go get incorporates GitHub.

➤ Go run builds and execute code in unison.

Chapter 2

Golang in Comparison to Other Languages

While Golang has many characteristics with other programming languages, it offers something different: Go's primary design objective, in contrast to certain other popular languages, is to enable quick compilation.

Java vs. Golang

Golang:

- ✓ Has memory management and trash collection built-in, making maintenance simpler for developers?
- ✓ Has a thriving and expanding ecosystem that offers a range of freely accessible tools and libraries.
- ✓ Provides developers with a community, copious documentation, and an easy-to-understand syntax that speeds up and simplifies writing.
- ✓ Facilitates effortless deployment across several platforms by supporting both compiled and interpreted deployment options.
- ✓ Has security features like tight type checking, memory safety, and secure code compilation built in.
- ✓ Consists of a growing array of third-party packages

for more specialized jobs and a vast library of standard packages for common tasks. It also features some well-known web frameworks, such as Echo and Gin.

✓ Use just-in-time compilation, is more compact and effective than Java, supports a wide range of operating systems natively, and compiles programs more quickly.

✓ Uses static typing, has quick compilation times, doesn't require interpreters or virtual machines, has elegant syntax, supports concurrency, and enables straightforward yet effective error handling.

Java

✓ It requires manual garbage collection and memory management; which developers need a lot of effort to maintain.

✓ Has a well-developed ecosystem with a vast library of available tools and libraries.

✓ It provides a verbose syntax that may be hard for novice developers to read and understand, along with scant documentation and an occasionally unhelpful community.

✓ needs to be compiled into a platform-specific

8

bytecode format before being deployed, which can take a while.

✓ Includes built-in security features including autonomous memory management, sandboxing, and bytecode verification.

✓ For more specialized activities, it offers a vast array of third-party libraries and frameworks in addition to a large library of standard packages for frequently used tasks. Three well-liked web frameworks are Hibernate, Struts, and Spring.

✓ Uses bytecode compilation, can compile more slowly than Golang, has to execute in a virtual machine or interpreter, and has a bigger memory footprint.

✓ Uses verbose syntax, requires manual memory management, requires a virtual machine or interpreter to execute, supports concurrency, and permits elaborate error handling.

C# vs. Golang

Golang

✓ Golang's straightforward syntax and comprehensive documentation make it comparatively simple to learn.

✓ Golang's low memory overhead and quick

compilation times translate into good performance.

✓ Web programming, concurrency, networking, data structures, and other functionalities are all included in the extensive standard library of Golang.

✓ Golang does not require an intermediate language such as Java bytecode or.NET Intermediate Language because it compiles directly to machine code.

✓ Golang is a cross-platform programming language compatible with Linux, Mac OS X, and Windows.

✓ Similar in syntax to C, Golang is a statically typed language that offers built-in concurrency primitives, garbage collection, and type safety.

C#

✓ C# performs well due to its Just-In-Time compilation and garbage collection.

✓ Because of its object-oriented design and comprehensive documentation, C# is a reasonably simple language to learn.

✓ Database access, networking, web programming, data structures, and other functionalities are all included in the extensive standard library of C#.

✓ Microsoft Intermediate Language (MSIL), which is compiled from C#, is subsequently compiled into native machine code during runtime.

✓ With a syntax akin to C++, C# is a statically typed object-oriented language that also has built-in language constructs for object-oriented programming and capabilities like garbage collection.

✓ The .NET framework can be implemented in an open-source manner to create cross-platform apps, but C# is a Windows-only language.

C++ vs. Golang

C++

✓ Excellent tooling for C++ includes a robust ecosystem of third-party tools and an integrated development environment (IDE).

✓ There is a sizable and vibrant community of C++ developers who actively contribute to the language.

✓ As long as programmers take care to write clear, organized code, C++ has good code quality.

✓ Because it can leverage low-level optimizations, C++ is fast and performs exceptionally well.

✓ For those who are not familiar with the language, learning C++ might be challenging, but there are many tools accessible.

11

✓ With a syntax like C, C++ is a feature-rich statically typed language.

Golang

✓ Golang boasts a robust ecosystem of third-party tools and an integrated development environment (IDE), among other good tooling.

✓ The Golang language is actively developed by numerous individuals and businesses. Developers can also find a wealth of materials and forums at their disposal.

✓ Because Golang encourages developers to write clear, organized code that is simple to understand and maintain, its code quality is quite high.

✓ Golang is renowned for its performance and speed. Its code can be compiled quickly, and its memory management system is quite effective.

✓ Particularly for developers accustomed to C-style languages, Golang is an easy language to learn. It also features a sizable library of packages and first-rate documentation.

✓ With a syntax akin to C, Golang is a statically typed language that also includes certain contemporary features like garbage collection and concurrency support.

Rust vs. Golang

Rust

- ✓ Creating a collection of tools for deployment, profiling, debugging, and development
- ✓ An expanding community with an increasing number of available libraries and frameworks
- ✓ Strong compiler checks and a type system result in high-quality code.
- ✓ It performs exceptionally well because of its ownership and borrowing arrangement and the absence of garbage collection.
- ✓ Because of its intricacy and inadequate documentation, it can be challenging to understand.
- ✓ Algebraic data types, pointer safety, ownership, and borrowing model, no garbage collection, concurrent support, static typing, and generics

Golang

- ✓ The comprehensive toolkit for development, profiling, debugging, and deployment
- ✓ A sizable, vibrant community offering an abundance

of libraries and frameworks
- ✓ Code that is easily accessible and follows a clear style guide
- ✓ Because trash collection and static typing are used, it performs well.

Chapter 3

The benefits of the Go language

Go simplifies the life of a developer in several ways.

Go is largely endorsed.

The Go toolchain can be downloaded for free as a Docker container or as a binary for Linux, MacOS, or Windows. Deploying Go source to well-known Linux distributions like Fedora and Red Hat Enterprise Linux is comparatively simpler because Go is pre-installed on those systems. Additionally, Go is well-supported by a wide range of third-party programming environments, such as ActiveState's Komodo IDE and Microsoft's Visual Studio Code.

Go is compatible.

Go accomplishes everything mentioned above without compromising system access. Go applications can call native system functions or communicate with external C libraries. For example, in Docker, Go communicates with low-level Linux namespaces, groups, and functions to perform container magic.

Go is handy.

Go's ability to meet a wide range of typical programming requirements has led to comparisons with scripting languages like Python. Goroutines, which allow for concurrency and threadlike behavior, are among the features that are integrated into the language itself. Other features can be found in Go standard library packages, such as the http package. Go offers automatic memory management features, such as garbage collection, just like Python.

Code written in Go compiles to a native binary that runs quickly, in contrast to scripting languages like Python. Additionally, Go compiles far faster than C or C++, so using Go seems more like using a scripting language than a compiled language. Moreover, compared to other compiled languages, the Go build method is simpler. Building and managing a Go project only requires a few steps and minimal paperwork.

It moves quickly.

Although Go binaries operate slower than C binaries, most programs don't notice the difference in speed. For most tasks, Go's performance is on par with C and typically far faster than other languages recognized for their rapid development (such as JavaScript, Python, and Ruby).

Go is portable.

Go toolchain-created executables are independent and don't require any external dependencies by default. The Go toolchain can be used to compile binaries across platforms and is compatible with a wide range of hardware devices and operating systems.

Wherever the Go language is most effective

Every language has its place in the workforce, although certain languages are more appropriate for certain vocations than others. The following application categories are where Go excels the most.

Standalone tools and utilities

Go programs require little external dependencies to compile into binaries. Their rapid startup time and easy packaging for redistribution make them perfect for developing utilities and other tools. Teleport, an access server (for SSH, among other things), is one example. Teleport may be quickly and simply installed on servers by downloading a prebuilt binary or constructing it from a source.

Network services that are distributed

Concurrency is the lifeblood of network applications, and Go's built-in concurrency features—mainly goroutines and channels—are ideal for this kind of work. Thus, networking, distributed processes, and cloud services are the focus of a large number of Go projects, which include web servers, APIs, basic frameworks for online applications, and similar projects.

Development using the cloud natively

Go's networking, parallelism, and high degree of portability make it an excellent choice for developing cloud-native applications. Docker, Kubernetes, and Istio are a few of the key components of cloud-native computing that were built with Go.

18

Go language restrictions

A common GUI toolkit is absent from Go.

The software development community still lacks a unified approach to creating sophisticated graphical user interfaces (GUIs) for desktop Go programs.

The majority of Go programs are either network services or command-line tools. Nevertheless, numerous initiatives aim to provide sophisticated graphical user interfaces for Go programs. The GTK and GTK3 frameworks have bindings. Platform-native user interfaces are the focus of another project; however, these are not developed entirely in Go and instead depend on C bindings. Users of Windows can also test out Walk. However, there is currently no apparent winner or safe long-term investment in this field, and several initiatives, like Google's effort to create a cross-platform GUI framework, have been shelved. Furthermore, it is doubtful that any of these will be included in the standard package collection because Go is platform-independent by design.

Lastly, even though Go can communicate with native system functions, it was not intended to be used for creating embedded systems or low-level system components like device drivers or kernels. After all, the underlying OS affects both the garbage collector for Go apps and the Go runtime. (Those looking for a state-of-the-art language for that kind of work may want to investigate the Rust language.)

Go leaves out a lot of language elements.

Go's opinionated feature set has garnered positive and negative feedback. Go intentionally omits several elements to err on the side of simplicity and ease of understanding. As a result, some capabilities that are standard in other languages are purposefully unavailable in Go.

A long-standing grievance was the absence of generic functions, which enable a function to take in a wide variety of variable types. Because they desired a syntax and set of behaviors that complemented the rest of Go, the Go development team resisted introducing generics to the language for a long time. However, a syntax for generics has been added to the language as of Go 1.18, which was published in early 2022. The important takeaway is that Go introduces significant features seldom and only after careful thought, to maintain wide version compatibility.

Go binaries have a lot of space.

One possible drawback of Go could be the size of the binaries that are produced. By default, Go binaries are statically constructed, which means that the binary image contains all of the resources required at runtime. This method makes the build and deployment process easier, but it comes with a price: on 64-bit Windows, a basic "Hello, world!" weighs about 1.5MB. With every new release, the Go team has been trying to make those binaries smaller. Go binaries can also be made smaller by deleting Go's debug information or by compressing them. This final solution might be more effective for distributed stand-alone applications than for cloud or network services, where debug information is helpful if a service malfunction.

Garbage collection consumes resources.

One potential disadvantage of Go's automated memory management functionality is that it necessitates some processing costs due to garbage collection. Go does not support manual memory management by design, and the garbage collection system in Go has come under fire for its inability to handle the types of memory loads found in corporate applications.

Nevertheless, the memory management features of Go appear to get better with each new release. For instance, trsh collection lag times were much reduced with Go 1.8. While manual memory allocation through a C extension or a third-party manual memory management library are options available to Go developers, most choose native solutions to those issues.

Chapter 4

Futures in the Go language

Instead of setting a rigid example, Go's minders are adapting the language to better suit the requirements and desires of its developer community, which will drive the language's future evolution. One example is the addition of generics to the language, which came about after extensive discussion about the most effective method to do it.

According to the 2021 Go Developer Survey, while most Go users were satisfied with the language's features, there was still much space for improvement. Dependency management—a persistent challenge in Go—diagnosing flaws, and dependability were the top areas where Go users sought improvements, with memory, CPU consumption, binary sizes, and build times ranking substantially lower.

A core collection of use cases is what most languages choose to focus on. In the ten years that it has been in business, Go has focused on network services, and it is expected to keep growing in this market. The creation of APIs or RPC services was, by far, the most common use case mentioned for the language (49%), followed by data processing (10%), web services (10%), and CLI applications (8%).

The fact that so many developers chose the Go language after testing it is another indication of its rising popularity. Of those surveyed who were thinking about taking on a project in Go, 75% selected the language. The most popular substitutes for Go among those who didn't select it were Rust (25%), Python (17%), and Java (12%). All those languages have found, or are finding, new uses: Python for automation, prototyping, and glue code; Java for corporate applications with a rich history; Rust for safe and quick systems development.

How quickly and easily Go can be developed for different use cases, as well as how deeply Go can permeate enterprise development, are yet unknown. However, Go's position as a leading programming language is already secure—at least in the cloud, where its simplicity and speed make it easier to create scalable infrastructure that will last over time.

Is Learning Golang Easy?

For programmers who are already familiar with C++ or Java, Go is a comparatively simple language to learn. Compared to many other programming languages, Go was intended to be a simple language with fewer features. Go places a strong emphasis on readability and simplicity, making its syntax likewise quite simple to comprehend.

Go's short, condensed standard library is one of the key factors making it simple to learn. It is simple to understand and use because the standard library has all the functions and data types that a developer could require. In addition, Go offers a comprehensive documentation library with a plethora of tutorials, examples, and other materials to aid developers in learning the language.

Go's garbage collector, which aids in memory management automatically, is another benefit. This gets rid of the necessity for manual memory management, which in other programming languages can lead to errors and defects. With Go, developers no longer have to worry about memory management and can concentrate on creating their applications.

Golang vs Python

Two well-known programming languages that are frequently contrasted are Python and Go. High-level and interpreted, Python is renowned for its user-friendliness and simplicity. It is frequently utilized in web development, scientific computing, and data analysis.

Conversely, Go is a low-level, compiled language with a focus on speed and efficiency. It is frequently employed in the construction of expansive, high-performing systems.

Even though each language has advantages, there are also significant distinctions between them. The fact that Python is an extremely beginner-friendly language is one of its key benefits. The grammar of Python is simple to read and comprehend, and there are lots of resources available to help with language acquisition. Furthermore, Python boasts a sizable and helpful community, making it simple for developers to get assistance when they need it.

Go, on the other hand, is perfect for developing high-performance systems since it is made to be quick and effective. Another benefit of Go is its support for concurrency, which makes it simpler to design programs that can manage several tasks at once. Additionally, Go features a modest standard library that facilitates learning and usage.

Ultimately, the needs of the project will determine whether to choose Go or Python. While Go is a strong option for developing large-scale, high-performance systems, Python is frequently a solid choice for novices, data analysis, and scientific computing.

In 2024, Is Golang Still Worth Learning?

Indeed, in 2024 it will be well worth knowing Golang. Over the past few years, Go has become more and more popular, and an increasing number of businesses are using it as their primary language. Go is very popular because it is fast and efficient, which makes it perfect for developing high-performance, large-scale systems.

Furthermore, Go boasts a multitude of features that make it an excellent choice for contemporary programming requirements, including strong concurrency support, an extensive standard library, and integrated garbage collection.

Numerous major digital businesses have also embraced Go, building their systems and tools with it, including Dropbox, Google, and Uber. This indicates that the need for Go developers is rising, making it a desirable skill to possess in the employment market.

Chapter 5

Top Reasons to Learn Golang

Developers may wish to learn Go for several reasons:

Community Open-Source

Since Go is an open-source language, programmers are welcome to contribute to the language community. Building sophisticated apps is now simpler with the abundance of libraries and tools the open-source community has produced for Go.

Simple to Implement

Go's short build times and straightforward syntax make it easier to launch apps quickly. Additionally, Go allows for cross-compilation, which enables the development of apps for several platforms using a single codebase.

Expanding Employment

Go engineers are in more demand as more businesses choose Go as their programming language. Gaining knowledge of Go can help developers remain competitive in the labor market and lead to new work prospects.

Scalability

Go's scalable architecture makes it the perfect choice for developing systems that must manage a large volume of requests. Go's ability to handle concurrency and manage memory effectively allows for the construction of extremely scalable systems.

Concurrency

Concurrency is supported natively in Go, which makes writing code that can manage several processes at once easier.

Compact Standard Library

Go's minimal standard library makes it simpler to use and learn. Without being overly comprehensive, the standard library has all the required functions and data types that a developer would require.

Elevated Efficiency

Go is perfect for developing high-performance, large-scale systems since it was created with performance in mind. It's a well-liked option for developing microservices and backend systems because of its easy syntax, quick compilation times, and integrated garbage collection

Why is Golang not as widely used as Java, Python, or JavaScript?

The ecosystems of Java, Python, and JavaScript are more developed than those of Go. This indicates that compared to the other languages, Go has fewer libraries, frameworks, and tools available. This may make it more challenging for developers to locate the materials required to create Go apps. The language Go is highly specialized. Go is meant for web development and systems programming, whereas Python, Java, and JavaScript are more all-purpose languages. This indicates that not all projects are a good fit for Go. For instance, Python is more widely used in data science and machine learning than Go.

The language Go is more recent. Given their lengthier lifespans, Python, Java, and JavaScript have had more opportunities to grow and amass a user base. Go hasn't had as much time to establish popularity as it has because it was only released in 2009. The learning curve in Go is steeper. Because Go is statically typed, developers must specify the kinds of data they use more precisely when working with it. For developers accustomed to languages with more dynamic typing, like Python or JavaScript, this may make learning more challenging.

Learning curve: Golang may be less approachable for novices due to its more difficult learning curve than certain other well-known languages.

For instance, Golang employs a distinct syntax for declarations and functions from other languages. Additionally, it makes extensive use of pointers, which can be perplexing to novice programmers.

Limited use cases: Certain applications, such as distributed systems and network programming, are ideally suited for Golang. Unlike Go, Python boasts a vast ecosystem of data science and machine learning libraries and tools. This implies that developing machine learning or data science applications in Go is more challenging. Go's web development environment is still expanding, but these languages have more expansive ecosystems of libraries and frameworks.

Saturation of the market: The problem of market saturation in Python and Java computer languages is complicated, and there isn't a universal solution. Nonetheless, a variety of elements might lead to market saturation, such as:

✓ The languages' level of popularity. Because Python and Java are two of the most widely used programming languages, many companies use them. It could be challenging for new companies to enter the market and increase their market share as a result.

✓ The resources' accessibility. Both Python and Java have a wealth of resources, including books, online groups, and tutorials. This facilitates the learning of programming languages and the creation of applications for developers.

✓ Programming languages are very competitively marketed, and languages like Python, Java, and JavaScript have already made a name for themselves as well-liked options for a variety of uses.

Goals of Golang

Go was developed to be effective. It was made to manage the enormous volume of independent, competitive requests that are sent to any program at the same time. Second, because of its straightforward syntax, it was also designed to improve a programmer's efficacy. It facilitates writing codes quickly and fluidly.

Golang has developed a common law format that enables program verification at any moment. Additionally, an erected-IDE tool that enables automated formatting is included. Moreover, it provides a simple and quick compilation, so you don't have to wait around for it to be built to see if your program functions. Since all of the laws in Go are centralized, anyone can work with dependencies while using the language.

Chapter 6

Golang Frameworks

Revel

Go-based Revel is a full-stack web framework with an emphasis on efficiency and speed. Routing, templating, asset packaging, session management, and an integrated testing environment are some of the features it offers. Support for the previously listed web services is also offered by Revel.

Echo

Go-based Echo is a high-performance web framework with an emphasis on productivity and speed. It offers functions including templating, session management, routing, middleware support, and an integrated testing environment. Web services including RESTful APIs, XML-RPC, and JSON-RPC are also supported by Echo.

Buffalo

Buffalo is a Go-based web framework designed to be developed quickly and efficiently. Routing, templating, asset packaging, session management, and an integrated testing environment are some of the features it offers. The same web services are supported by Buffalo as well.

Beego

Beego is an additional Go-based web framework that aims to be quick, adaptable, and simple to use. Routing, templating, session management, and an integrated testing environment are among the features it offers. Beego supports web services, including RESTful APIs, XML-RPC, and JSON-RPC.

Gin

Gin is a lightweight, speedy, and feature-rich Go web framework. Because of its straightforward design and ease of use, it's perfect for developers who wish to quickly create web apps. In addition, it offers functions like templating, routing, middleware support, and an integrated testing environment.

Why Golang is now the preferred language for microservices

Golang is quickly becoming the preferred language for microservices. Because of its application in creating distributed systems, it has become a desirable choice for businesses looking to develop applications and services quickly and effectively.

To begin with, Golang is an easy-to-learn and use statically typed and compiled language. This makes it a very easy-to-understand and maintain language, which is perfect for building microservices.

Furthermore, Golang offers a feature-rich feature set that makes it an excellent choice for developing microservices. These characteristics consist of an integrated garbage collector, a lightweight runtime, and concurrency support. Secondly, Golang is a cross-platform language compatible with various architectures and operating systems.

Because of this, it is perfect for developing distributed systems that must be cross-platform compatible. Microservices may be easily deployed across several environments thanks to Golang's cross-platform capability, which enables developers to swiftly transfer their code to numerous platforms.

Golang is quick. Because of the language's quick and effective architecture, programmers can produce high-performing apps. Static typing in the language also increases the likelihood of fast and effective code execution. Because of this, Golang is the best language to use when developing microservices that must process large amounts of requests quickly.

And lastly, Golang has great scalability. Because of the language's capability for horizontal scaling, developers can quickly add more nodes to their distributed system without having to change the code. This ensures that applications stay responsive even under high load by making it simple to scale up microservices as demand grows.

To sum up, Golang's straightforward syntax, extensive feature set, cross-platform compatibility, speed, and scalability make it a great option for developing microservices. Because of its use in distributed systems, it is a well-liked option for developers who want to swiftly and effectively design services and applications. Golang is the preferred language for microservices because of these factors.

Conclusion

Go, sometimes referred to as Golang, is a potent programming language that's perfect for creating complex, high-performing systems. It's a favorite among developers because of its support for concurrency, effective memory management, and straightforward syntax.

Go engineers are in more demand as more businesses choose Go as their programming language. Learning Go can help you stay competitive in the job market and open up new work options, regardless of your level of expertise as a developer.